OBEDIENCE

RANIERO CANTALAMESSA

OBEDIENCE

The authority of the Word

 St Paul Publications

Original title: *L'Obbedienza*
Copyright © Editrice Ancora Milano, 1986

Translated from the Italian by Frances Lonergan Villa

Cover design by Mary Lou Winters, FSP

St Paul Publications
Middlegreen, Slough SL3 6BT, England

English translation copyright © St Paul Publications 1989
First published in Great Britain 1989
Typeset by Society of St Paul, Maynooth, Ireland
Printed by Billing and Sons, Worcester
ISBN 085439 281 5

St Paul Publications is an activity of the priests and brothers of
the Society of St Paul who proclaim the Gospel through the
media of social communication.

CONTENTS

1. A RENEWAL OF OBEDIENCE 'IN THE SPIRIT"

Chapter 13 of the Letter to the Romans opens with a well-known text on obedience: 'Everyone is to obey the governing authorities, because there is no authority except from God and so whatever authorities exist have been appointed by God. So anyone who disobeys an authority is rebelling against God's ordinance' (Rm 13:1ff).

Like other passages of the New Testament (Tt 3:1; 1 P 2:13-15) the remainder of the passage, where the sword and taxes are spoken of, clearly shows that the Apostle is not talking about authority in general, or just about any kind of authority, but exclusively about state and civil authority. His aim is to give Christians some guidelines on the best way to live their Christian calling in society. Some very reliable modern translations of the Bible (such as the recent combined version by the Catholic and Lutheran Churches of Germany) stress this sense of the text very opportunely: 'Everyone is to obey the state authorities, because there is no state authority except from God'. After all, this is how this text was understood by the Fathers of the Church at the beginning, when the political authority to which St Paul refers was still in power.[1] Later, however, it was willingly extended, in fact and in practice, to every kind of authority, so much so that in many manuals it became the very basis and, so to say, the 'Magna Charta' of Christian obedience.

But, even when limited to civil authority, the Pauline text has never failed to deeply disturb those who have tried to take it seriously, especially after Luther used it as the basis for his theory on the 'two kingdoms'. This theory places civil authority and the Church on the same level, as one of the two ways, different but equally important, through which God governs and directly rules the things of the world. In fact, seen in this light, the text of Romans 13 creates what has been called 'the fatal point of compromise between faith and this world' (M. Dibelius), opening the way to the kind of metaphysics which, in modern times, has often led to civil authority being idealised and made absolute with fatal results. How is it possible to affirm that 'every state authority' comes from God and that to rebel against it is to rebel against God, without thus bringing to a sudden halt the whole course of history and the very behaviour of Christians up to our time, or making it incomprehensible? And how could such a view be

[1] St Irenaeus, *Adv. Haer.* V, 24.1-4; Origen, *Comm. in Rom.*; cf. PG 14, 1226.

reconciled with the equally authoritative one of Revelation 13, where it is clearly stated that the same political power 'in fact existing' (which is the Roman Empire) gets its power from Satan? Would this not be to confer on secular power – even when this itself is conceived without God, or against God – a dangerous religious basis, binding on conscience, which could be put to rather dangerous use? It is everyday news that officials of political regimes, when brought to justice, justify killings, torture and ill-treatment of all kinds by saying they were obeying a 'superior authority'.

Indeed, I am convinced that this difficulty cannot be overcome, unless Paul's text is considered in the light of what he said earlier about obedience. It shall not be used as a basis for obedience but seen as it really is, as a particular case within the sphere of another much more essential obedience, that is, 'obedience to the Gospel'. We must therefore look at Christian obedience from other stand points which, as we shall see, also enable us to understand this well-known text.

There is in fact a type of obedience which concerns everyone, superiors and subjects alike, religious and lay people. This is the most important of all and it rules and gives life to all other types of obedience. It is not the obedience of 'man to man' but the obedience of man to God. And this is the obedience we want to discover, or rediscover, in St Paul and in the whole Bible. Obedience to God is like 'the thread on high' which supports a splendid spider's web hanging from a bush. The little spider itself has made this thread and going down it has woven the whole cobweb which is now perfect and tautly stretched at every angle. Yet when the job is terminated the spider does not destroy the thread from which it built the web: the thread remains. It is actually this which, from the centre, supports the whole web and without which the whole thing could collapse. If any part of the web happens to become damaged, the spider immediately sets about repairing it, but as soon as this thread from on high is cut, the spider moves off as if there was nothing more to be done about it. Something similar happens with regard to authority and obedience in society, in a religious order, in the Church. Obedience to God is the thread from on high. Everything was built starting from this, but this thread cannot be forgotten, not even when the building is finished. Otherwise, everything falls back on itself and collapses.

When considering obedience, it is necessary to make a recapitulation according to the classic meaning given to this word by St Irenaeus: 'take things at their *origin*, leading them to *unity*'. St Irenaeus is of great help to us in this undertaking. He shows particular feeling for the theme of obedience and has at the same time the advantage of approaching Scripture with, so to say, virgin eyes, without the filter of those particular interpretations of obedience which came later. He represents the oldest stage of the tradition on obedience, that which is closest to the source. In fact, the forms and characteristics which obedience assumed later on in the life of the Church are numerous. There has been an ecclesiastical obedience and a monastic obedience. Within the monastic obedience, there has been a Basilian type of obedience, a Pacomian type of obedience and a Benedictine type of obedience. In mediaeval times we have Franciscan obedience, connected with poverty, which insists on the importance of the denial of one's own will, and a Dominican obedience, more open to the apostolate, which gives more importance to the 'common good' reached through the union of wills. With St Ignatius of Loyola, there was emphasis on the radicalism of obedience ('blind, like a cadaver'). Nowadays, since the Council, we like to speak of responsible obedience, obedience through dialogue or charitable obedience. All these kinds of obedience, in their own environments and times, have been authentic expressions of the vitality of the Church and have given rise to a marvellous flourishing of works and sanctity. But, just as in February to March the fruit-tree is pruned of the previous season's branches – even if it was a good season, and is thus reduced to a trunk or little more, so that the lymph can gather and the tree be made ready for a new flowering in spring, – so, at every turning in the life of the

Church, the word of God must be laid bare so as to make a new spring and a new fruit season possible.

These images of pruning and of a new spring are not mine; they were first used by Pope Paul VI in his opening speech of the second session of the Council.[2] But a spiritual spring can only come about through the work of the Holy Spirit. In fact, the image of a 'new spring' only re-expresses the idea dear to Pope John XXIII of a 'New Pentecost' for the Church. It is the Holy Spirit who 'renews the face of the earth'. A Father of the Church once said: 'As in spring the blowing of a warm west wind causes buds to spring up everywhere and the fields exude the sweet scent of spring blossoms, ... so through the miraculous work of the Holy Spirit, beautiful flowers are born in the Church.'[3] On the anniversary of the sixteenth centenary of the First Ecumenical Council of Constantinople – the Council that defined the divinity of the Holy Spirit – Pope John Paul II very truly wrote that 'the whole *work of renewal in the Church*, which Vatican Council II so providentially proposed and started ... cannot be fulfilled if not *in the Holy Spirit*, that is, with the help of his light and strength'.[4]

This principle holds also for the renewal of

---

[2] *AAS* 55, 1963, pp. 850ff.
[3] Cf. St Zeno of Verona, *Tract.* I, 33; CC 22, p. 84.
[4] *AAS* 73, 1981, p. 512.

obedience. It has been written that, 'If obedience constitutes a problem today, it is not one of docility to the Holy Spirit – on whom, indeed, all seem willing to call – but rather that of submission to a hierarchy, to a humanly expressed law or authority'. I am myself convinced that this is the case. But it is precisely in order to make this real obedience to law and visible authority possible and flourishing again that we must start from obedience to God and his Spirit. I mean, from *true* obedience to the Spirit and not an obedience simply *presumed* as such, which would, effectively, change nothing. Obedience is not in fact renewed by law, but by grace; not by the letter, but by the Spirit. When he came into the world, Jesus did not renew human obedience by strengthening or perfecting existing laws – even if he also did this – but by giving, at Pentecost, a new and interior law, thus fulfilling the prophecy which says: I shall put my spirit in you, and make you keep my laws and respect and practise my judgements (Ezk 36:27). It is the Spirit therefore – that is, Grace – which alone can give man both the command and the capacity to obey 'laws and statutes'. It is therefore to the Spirit that we entrust ourselves, so that he may take us by the hand and guide us in our quest to rediscover the great secret of obedience.

2. THE OBEDIENCE
OF CHRIST

It is relatively easy to discover the nature and origin of Christian obedience: it is sufficient to understand which concept of obedience is used in Scripture to define Jesus as 'the obedient'. It is thus immediately obvious that the true basis of Christian obedience is not an idea of obedience, but an act of obedience; it is not a principle ('the inferior must be subject to the superior'), but an event; it is not founded upon a 'constitutional natural order', but in itself constitutes a new order; it is not found in reason *(recta ratio)*, but in the kerygma. It is based on the fact that 'Christ became obedient even unto death' (Ph 2:8); that Christ 'learnt to obey through suffering and having been made perfect he became for all who obey him the source of eternal salvation' (cf. Heb 5:8-9). The luminous focus, which sheds light on the whole discourse on obedience in the Letter to the Romans, is Rm 5:19: 'By one man's obedience are many to be made upright'. The obedience of Christ is the immediate and the historical source of justification; both are closely connected. Anyone who recognises the importance of justification in the Letter to the Romans can understand the importance of obedience in this text. In the New Testament, the obedience of Christ is not only the most sublime *example* of obedience, but it is its very *foundation*. It is the 'constitution' of the Kingdom of God!

Let us try to understand the nature of that 'act' of obedience on which the new order is built; let us try, in other words, to understand what the obedience of Christ consisted in. Jesus, as a child, obeyed his parents. Then, as an adult, he submitted himself to the Mosaic Law, to the Sanhedrin, to Pilate... But St Paul is not thinking of any of these obediences; he is thinking instead of Christ's obedience to the Father. The obedience of Christ is, in fact, considered to be the exact antithesis of the disobedience of Adam: 'As by one man's disobedience many were made sinners, so by one man's obedience are many to be made upright' (Rm 5:19; cf. 1 Co 15:22). Also in the hymn of the Letter to the Philippians the obedience of Christ 'even to death and death on a cross' is tacitly contraposed to the disobedience of Adam who wants to be 'equal with God' (cf. Ph 2:6ff). But who was it that Adam disobeyed? Certainly not his parents, a government, laws... He disobeyed God. Disobedience to God is at the root of every disobedience and obedience to God is at the root of every obedience. St Francis says that the disobedience of Adam consisted in appropriating his own will to himself: 'He who appropriates to himself his own will eats from the tree of good and evil'.[1] By contrast we can understand what the obedience of the new Adam consisted in. He gave up his own will, he emptied himself (*ekenosen*): 'Not my will but thine be done', he exclaimed to the Father (cf. Lk 22:42); and again: 'I have come not to do my own will, but to do the will of the one who sent me' (Jn 6:38).

St Irenaeus interprets Christ's obedience in the light of the Songs of the Servant as an interior, absolute submission to God, carried out in an extremely difficult situation. 'That sin', he writes, 'which came about on wood was abolished by the obedience of wood because in obeying God, the Son of man was nailed to wood, thus destroying the science of evil and introducing the science of good into the world. Evil is disobedience to God, just as obedience to God is the good. Thus says the Word, through the prophet Isaiah: "I have not resisted and I have not turned away. I have offered my back to those who struck me, my cheeks to those who plucked my beard. I have not turned my face away from insult and spitting" (Is 50:5-6). Therefore, by virtue of that obedience unto death hanging from a cross, he dissolved the ancient disobedience which came about on wood.'[2] The antithesis 'disobedience-obedience' is, as we can see, so radical and universal

---

[1] *Admonition* II.
[2] *Epid*. 34.

for St Irenaeus as to be equivalent to the opposition between good and evil: Evil, he says, is disobeying God and obeying God is the good.

Obedience encompasses the whole life of Jesus. If St Paul and the Letter to the Hebrews give importance to the place of obedience in the death of Jesus (cf. Ph 2:8; Heb 5:8), St John and the synoptics complete the picture by giving importance to the place obedience played daily in the life of Jesus. 'My food', says Jesus in John's Gospel, 'is to do the will of the Father'; and again: 'I always do what pleases him' (Jn 4:34; 8:29).

The obedience of Jesus Christ to the Father is carried out above all through obedience to the written word. When Jesus was tempted in the desert, his obedience consisted in recalling the word of God and keeping to it. 'It is written!' God's words, under the present action of the Holy Spirit, become vehicles of the living will of God and reveal their 'binding' nature as orders from God. Herein lies the obedience of the new Adam in the desert. After the last 'It is written' said by Jesus, Luke goes on to tell us that the 'devil left him' (Lk 4:12) and that Jesus returned to Galilee 'filled with the Holy Spirit' (Lk 4:14). The Holy Spirit is given to those who 'obey God' (Ac 5:32). St James says: 'Give in to God, resist the devil, and he will run away from you' (Jm 4:7). That is what happened when Jesus was tempted. Jesus bases his obedience, in a particular way, on the words written about him and for him 'in the law, in the prophets and in the psalms', which he, as man, gradually discovers as he advances in understanding and fulfilling his mission. The perfect concord that exists between the prophecies of the Old Testament and the acts of Jesus, as seen in the New Testament, cannot be explained by saying that the prophecies depend on the acts (that is, that the prophecies were later applied to the acts already carried out by Jesus) but by saying that the acts depend on the prophecies: Jesus 'fulfilled' in perfect obedience what was written of him by the Father. When his disciples want to oppose his capture, Jesus says: 'But then how would the scriptures be fulfilled that say this is the way it must be?' (Mt 26:54). The life of Jesus seems to be guided by an invisible luminous trail formed of the words written for him; it is from the Scriptures that he takes the 'must be' (*dei*) which governs his whole life.

The greatness of the obedience of Jesus is measured *objectively* 'by what he suffered' and *subjectively* by the love and freedom with which he obeyed. St Basil says there are three dispositions with which one can obey: the first is a fear of punishment, as in the case with slaves; the second is a desire for reward, as in the case of mercenaries; the third one is out of love and this is the attitude of sons and daughters.[3] Filial obedience is radiant in Jesus to

---

[3] Cf. St Basil, *Reg. Fus. Proem*. PG 31, 896.

the highest and most perfect degree. Even in the most extreme moments, as when the Father offers him the chalice of the passion to drink, this filial cry 'Abba!' was always on his lips. 'My God, my God, why have you abandoned me?' he exclaimed from the cross (Mt 27:46); but, according to Luke, he immediately added: 'Father, into your hands I commend my spirit' (Lk 23:46). On the cross Jesus abandoned himself to the God who was abandoning him! This is what obedience unto death means; this is the 'rock of our salvation'.

In the obedience of Jesus, as seen in the New Testament, it is possible to grasp the fullest and deepest meaning of this virtue. It is not only a *moral* virtue, but a *theological* one also. From the Scholastic viewpoint, which was based on schemes of virtues taken from Aristotle and Stoicism, obedience is connected with justice; as such, it is placed among the moral virtues whose object is the means, not the end, and it is strictly distinct from the theological virtues – faith, hope, charity – through which one adheres to God himself. But in the Bible, and especially in the New Testament, obedience, in so far as it is principally obedience to God, is above all so connected with faith as often to be confused with it. It concerns therefore not only the means but also the end; through it one adheres to God himself and not simply to an intermediate good, even if this is the 'common good'. 'It was by faith that Abraham obeyed the call' (Heb 11:8). Obedience is the type of faith required when the revealed word is not simply a *truth* of God to be believed, but the *will* of God to be fulfilled. Faith, in another sense, is also obedience when it manifests itself as a truth to be believed, because reason does not accept it for its intrinsic *evidence*, but because of the *authority* behind it. The expression, 'obedience to faith', which we often find in St Paul, does not simply mean obeying what is believed, but rather to obey believing, by the very fact of believing. St Irenaeus expresses this very concisely when he says that 'believing is to do God's will'.[4] The very words in which obedience is expressed are closely connected to those used to express faith: one term (*hypakuo, ob-audire*), in fact, means to listen and another term (*peithomai*, from the same root as *pistis!*) means to let oneself be persuaded, to have faith in or trust in.

Furthermore, from the word of God we learn that the virtue of obedience is more positive than negative. Here too, with the passing of time and with the prevailing of ascetic interest over the mysteric and kerygmatic, obedience is above all seen as a negative virtue or one of denial. Its pre-eminence among the virtues is derived from the importance of the good that is renounced through it, that is, one's own will.

---

[4] *Adv. Haer.* IV, 6, 5.

This good is greater than all the exterior things one renounces through poverty, greater than one's body, renounced through chastity. But in biblical terms, the positive aspect – to do the will of God – is more important than the negative aspect – not to do one's own will. Jesus says: 'Not my will but thine be done' (the emphasis being on the second part); 'My food is to do the will of the Father!' and, again, 'Here I am! I am coming to do your will' (Heb 10:2). Salvation, in fact, comes from doing the will of God, not from not doing one's own will. In the 'Our Father' we ask that 'Thy will be done'; we are asking for something positive. In the Scriptures we read that God wants obedience, not sacrifice (cf. 1 S 15:22; Heb 10:5-7). We know, nonetheless, that he also wants sacrifice in the case of Christ and that he wants it from us too… The explanation lies in the fact that of the two things, one is the means, the other the end. God wants obedience for itself whereas he wants sacrifice only indirectly, in relation to the first. The sentence therefore means: what God seeks, in sacrifice, is obedience! The sacrifice of one's own will is the means for conforming to the divine will. To those who were scandalised at how God could find pleasure in the sacrifice of his Son Jesus, St Bernard rightly replies: 'It was not the death that pleased him but the will of him who spontaneously died!'[5] It is not so much therefore the

---

[5] *De errore Abelardi* 8, 21; cf. PL 182, 1070.

death of Christ that saved us, as his *obedience* unto death.

It is true that the two things – 'not to do one's own will' and 'to do the will of God' – are strictly interdependent. They are not, however, identical and neither do they have the same limits. Not to do one's own will is not always, in itself, a saving factor, whereas doing the will of God is. The positive reason for obedience goes much further than the negative one. God can ask things not with the aim of making us deny our own will, but to test and increase our faith and charity. The Bible defines the act that led Abraham to immolate his son as obedience (cf. Gn 22:18), even if the aim was not to make Abraham deny his will, but to test his faithfulness. The aim of all is in fact to get human freedom to return freely to adhering to God, so that only one will, God's will, may reign again in the universe as was the case before sin appeared. Through obedience we have, in some way, 'the return of creatures to God'. At the head of all biblical motivations for obedience, higher than faith itself, there is charity. Obedience is the nuptial 'yes' of the creature to the Creator, in which the final union of the two wills, the essence of eternal bliss, is, however imperfectly, already at work. 'It is through obedience', a Father of the desert said, 'that we are not only in the image of God but like to God'.[6] We are in

[6] Diadochus Phot., *Cap. gnost.* 4; S. Ch. 5, p. 86.

the image of God through the very fact of our existence, but through our obedience to him we are like to him, as through obedience we conform ourselves to his will and, through our free choice, become what he is by nature. We are like to God because we want what he wants.

3. OBEDIENCE AS GRACE: BAPTISM

In Chapter 5 of the Letter to the Romans, St Paul presents Christ as the 'head' of the obedient, in contrast to Adam who was the 'head' of the disobedient. As we have said, Christ's obedience, in life and in death, constitutes the new basis and the criterion on which the virtue of obedience is founded. In the chapter that follows, the Apostle reveals how we come to be part of the event, through baptism. As always, through the *sacrament* we come in contact with the *event*. We could compare Christ's obedience to a powerful waterfall which has put an immense power-station into action; it is the starting wire of a current of energy that flows throughout history in the Church. But the presence of an electric wire is not sufficient to give power and light to a house; the wire must be connected. On a spiritual level this comes about in baptism. Baptism is the moment in which each individual enters into contact with the current of grace coming from the paschal mystery of Christ and a new life is 'switched on' in him.

Baptism has an exceptional significance in Christian obedience which has almost been lost sight of in catechesis. St Paul first of all lays down a principle: if you freely place yourself under the jurisdiction of someone, you are then bound to serve and obey him: 'You know well that if you undertake to be somebody's slave and obey him, you are the slave of him you obey: you can be the slave of either sin which leads to death, or of Obedience which leads to saving justice' (Rm 6:16). (In this quotation, I have used a capital letter for obedience, because we are no longer dealing with abstract obedience but with the obedience of Christ, or simply, of the obedient Christ). Now, once the principle has been established, St Paul recalls the event. Christians, in fact, freely place themselves under the jurisdiction of Christ on the day when, through baptism, they accept him as their Lord. 'Once you were slaves of sin, but thank God you have given whole-hearted obedience to the pattern of teaching to which you were introduced; and so, being freed from serving sin, you took uprightness as your master' (Rm 6:17). With baptism there has been a changeover of master, a changeover of sides: from sin to justice, from disobedience to obedience, from Adam to Christ. The Liturgy expresses all of this in the contrasting 'I renounce – I believe', statements. In ancient times dramatic gestures were used in some baptism rituals to make this interior event visible. The one being baptised first turned towards the west, considered the symbol of darkness, and made signs repudiating and banishing Satan and all his works; then he turned towards the east, the symbol of light, and bowing deeply saluted Christ as his new Lord, as if he were a soldier abandoning the tyrant's army for that of the liberator in a war between two kingdoms.

Therefore, in Christian life obedience is something essential; it is the practical and necessary turning-point in accepting the lordship of Christ. There can be no lordship in action without man's obedience. In baptism we accepted a Lord, a *Kyrios*, but an 'obedient' Lord, one who became Lord precisely because of his obedience (cf. Ph 2:8-11), one whose lordship, so to say, consists in obedience. Obedience, from this point of view, is not so much subjection as likeness. To obey such a Lord is to be like him, because he, too, obeyed. We find a splendid confirmation of the Pauline thought on this point in Peter's First Letter. The faithful — the Letter tells us at the beginning — 'have been chosen in the foresight of God the Father, to be made holy by the Spirit, obedient to [= in order to obey] Jesus Christ' (1 P 1:2). Christians were chosen and sanctified 'to obey'; the Christian calling is a call to obedience! A little further on in the same Letter, the faithful are defined rather suggestively as 'sons of obedience': 'Do not allow yourselves to be shaped by the passions of your old ignorance, but as obedient children' *(tekna hypakoes)* (1 P 1:14). It is not sufficient to translate this expression 'obedient sons' (as if we were dealing with a simple hebraism), because here, as the context clearly shows, the reference is to baptism. 'Sons of obedience' is equivalent to 'sanctified by obedience' which immediately follows in the text (cf. 1 P 1:22). The context is not, therefore, ascetic, but mysteric; the Apostle is talking about 'a new birth from the word of God' (cf. 1 P 1:23). Christians are children of obedience, because they are born as such from the obedience of Christ and from their own decision to obey Christ. Like little fish born in water who cannot survive out of water, so Christians, born in obedience, can live spiritually only through obedience, that is, in a state of constant and loving submission to God, in contact with the paschal mystery of Christ. The sacramental link with Christ's obedience does not end, in fact, with baptism, but is daily renewed in the Eucharist. When celebrating Holy Mass, we recall – and more than recall – the obedience of Christ unto death. We put on obedience as a mantle of justice and thus arrayed we present ourselves to the Father as 'children of obedience'. In receiving the Body and Blood of Christ, we nourish ourselves with his obedience.

From this we discover that obedience, before being a virtue, is a gift, and before being law, it is grace. The difference is that the law tells us to do something, while grace makes it possible for us to do it. Obedience is above all the work of God in Christ, which is then pointed out to the believer, so that he, in turn, will faithfully imitate it in his life. In other words, we are not just obliged to obey but we also have the grace to obey!

Christian obedience is, therefore, rooted in baptism; through baptism all Christians are 'vowed' to obedience; they have, in a certain sense, made a 'vow' of obedience. For centuries, before the idea of religious 'vows' or the religious 'state' was affirmed (this came about in the late Middle Ages), the reason for which one entered the consecrated life was to be able better and more thoroughly to observe the demands of Christian life. St Basil simply called monks 'Christians'. In his day (as is happening again in our day!) the really important distinction was not that between monks and the rest of the Christian community, but the distinction between this community, taken as a whole, and the external world which did not live according to the Gospel.[1] The word of God urges us today to rediscover what is common to all Christians; it urges us to seek again what unites more than what divides. This is true not only of the relations among the various Churches, but also of categories within the same Church. What unites us is, in fact, the essence, while the way of living only distinguishes us.

The rediscovery of fundamental obedience is of enormous help to religious people them-

---

[1] St Basil, *Reg. Fus.* 22; cf PG 31, 977.

selves. Today they are becoming ever more aware of the fact that a renewal of obedience depends neither on constantly perfecting their rules and constitutions, not even on a return to their sources (if this means the sources of their particular religious order), but it comes only from the Spirit working in the Word and in the sacraments: it comes from a return to the source of sources, that is, to Christ. 'The law', St John says, 'was given through Moses, grace and truth have come through Jesus Christ' (Jn 1:17). These words still hold true and mean that the *law*, or the rule, to obey was given to us by Basil, or Benedict, or Francis, or Ignatius, or Theresa...: but that the *grace* to obey is given to us, as to them, only by Jesus Christ. St Paul says that it is not being circumcised or uncircumcised that counts, but being 'new creatures' (Ga 6:15). In the same way it is not being lay or cleric, or belonging to one religious order rather than another that counts, but being new creatures. All the rest counts – and very much so – if this exists; otherwise, it is of no value. Colours exist and they are wonderful, but only if there is light to colour them...

The rediscovery of this biblical idea, founded on baptism, meets the most important needs of the *laity* in the Church. Vatican Council II announced the principle of a 'universal call to holiness' of the people of God (cf. *Lumen Gentium* 40) and, as there is no sanctity without obedience, to say that all those baptised are called to holiness is to say that all are called to obedience… However, it is now necessary that those baptised be offered a type of holiness and obedience made to their measure, without a particular character, state or tradition attached to it which would be too far from their way of life. And this holiness, objectively seen, can be nothing other than that essential holiness traced out by the word of God and founded on baptism. St Paul, in his exhortation, outlines a life of the highest perfection made up of charity, humility, service, purity, sacrifice, obedience but which is derived from nothing other than baptism.

4. OBEDIENCE AS 'DUTY': THE MEANING OF ROMANS 13:1-7

In the first part of the Letter to the Romans, St Paul presents Jesus Christ to us as a 'gift' to be accepted with faith, while in the second or parenthetical part, he presents Christ as a 'model' to imitate in life. Two aspects of salvation are also present within the single virtues or fruits of the Spirit. In every Christian virtue there is a mysteric and an ascetic element, a part entrusted to grace and another part entrusted to freedom. There in an 'impressed' obedience in us and an obedience 'expressed' by us. Now it is time to consider this second aspect, that is, our actual imitation of Christ's obedience, obedience as a duty. Thanks to the coming of Christ, the law became 'grace', but later on, thanks to the coming of the Holy Spirit, grace became 'law', the new 'law of the Spirit'.

Going through the New Testament, trying to find out what the duty of obedience consists in, it is surprising to discover that obedience is almost always obedience to God. All the other forms of obedience are certainly spoken of: obedience to parents, masters, superiors, governing powers, 'to every human institution' (1 P 2:13), but much less so and much less solemnly. The noun 'obedience' (*hypakoe*) – which is the strongest term – is used always and only to indicate obedience to God or, at any rate, to instances which are connected with God, except in one passage in the Letter to Philemon, where it indicates obedience to the Apostle. St Paul speaks of obedience to *faith* (Rm 1:5; 16:26), of obedience to the *teaching* (Rm 6.17), of obedience to the *Gospel* (Rm 10:16; 2 Th 1:8), of obedience to *truth* (Ga 5:7), of obedience to *Christ* (2 Co 10:5). We also find the same language elsewhere: the Acts of the Apostles speak of obedience to faith (Ac 6:7), the First Letter of Peter speaks of obedience to Christ (1 P 1:2) and of obedience to truth (1 P 1:22).

We can easily understand what all these expressions mean if we start from the passage to the Galatians: 'You began your race well, who came to obstruct you and stop you obeying the truth?' (Ga 5:7). The Apostle is speaking to Judaizers, that is, to those who made of the Law of Moses and its ordinances an ideal they could not give up. Therefore, what does the statement that the Galatians 'do not obey the truth' mean? It means that they obey the law rather than the Gospel. Truth, faith, the Gospel, Christ are all expressions indicating the same reality. Their common characteristic is that they are of divine and not of human authority. A new will of God was manifested in Christ, which is the fulfilment of all the preceding ones; to go on obeying the old order is, now, to disobey. To keep to the old obedience would be like a novice who, having received an order from his superior at the beginning of his novitiate, goes on carrying out that order for the rest of his life in spite of the fact that it is the superior himself who now asks him to change and do something else. Obedience to truth is obedience to what is new, obedience to the 'new' Testament.

With this framework it is possible to explain the much disputed text of Romans 13:1-7 on obedience to state authority. It is now time for us to examine this text again, even if this will momentarily interrupt the spiritual tone of our reflections. St Paul, like the other Apostles, came from a Jewish background with all the problems and the mentality of that world. This is shown by his constant reference to the situation of Israel in his Letter to the Romans. The Jews are his kinsmen by flesh. He sees the world through Jewish eyes, even if now enlightened by Christ. It is simply unthinkable that around 58 AD, he could have spoken of the existing state authority (because this is what he is speaking of!), without considering the extremely difficult situation which then existed in the Jewish world. It was the time when the open revolt against Rome, headed by the Zealots, was growing, and was to lead to the destruction of Jerusalem. The hypothesis that the Apostle spoke these words about the state simply to restrain 'enthusiastic' Christians who believed themselves dispensed from all dependence (a hypothesis, that is, that Paul was fighting only a false idea of Christian liberty) is not a satisfactory explanation. We find the same ideas in other texts of the New Testament where the background is certainly not that of an enthusiastic Church but that of a persecuted Church. The words of the Apostle – like the analogous ones in the First Letter of Peter (2:13) – are dictated by a pastoral concern more than anything else. The problem was to place the young Christian community outside a conflict which would have irremediably compromised its peace and its universal character. The Apostle invites the Christians to pray for the king and for those in power 'so that we may live a calm and tranquil life' (1 Tm 2:2).

The obedience to the state urged by Paul is of the same order and can be explained in the same terms as the obedience towards their masters recommended to slaves: 'Slaves, be obedient in every way to the people who, according to human reckoning, are your masters' (Col 3:22).

In the First Letter of Peter the two obediences are mentioned one after the other as if part of the same fundamental duty: 'For the sake of the Lord, accept the authority of ever human institution: the emperor, as the supreme authority, and the governors... Slaves, you should obey your masters respectfully' (1 P 2:13-18). This second obedience, too, is said to be the 'will of God' and must be done 'whole-heartedly' and not by force (cf. Ep 6:5-6). Slavery is an accepted thing in this passing world (cf. 1 Co 7:20-24.31), as something the Church found present right from the beginning, just as it found the Roman state – and which, given its actual possibilities and the priority of its spiritual task, it does not feel called to discuss and change, at least for the moment. But it no longer means the same thing, because in the new order established by Christ, there is a new type of freedom and slavery, or obedience, with regard to which masters and slaves are both on the same level and both receive the same inheritance (cf. 1 Co 12:13; Ga 3:28; Ep 6:5-9; Col 3:11-24). This does not mean that Paul puts the state on the same level as slavery. It just means that the Apostle considers the state from the same point of view as he considers slavery, that is, from the new situation created by the coming of the lordship of Christ, without going into the specific merits of their nature or legitimacy. What Paul really wishes to make clear is that it is possible to belong to the community of salvation, even in submission to masters and governing powers; actually, this is required in the interests of the whole community.

It would seem to me most important to stress that in taking this attitude on obedience to a foreign political power the Apostle enters into a precise *prophetic tradition* which concerns the attitude towards Babylonian power at the time of exile. If it is true, therefore, as has been pointed out, that in our text Paul uses profane, Hellenistic-Roman language to express himself concerning the state, it must be underlined that 'profane' and 'Hellenistic-Roman' apply only to the language, while the basic idea is, on the contrary, exquisitely biblical. We cannot but see a relationship between Paul's words in Romans 13:1-7 and those addressed by God to the people, through Jeremiah, just before the exile: '*I* by my great power and outstretched arm made the earth, the human beings and the animals that are on earth, and I give them to whom I please. For the present, I have handed all these countries over to Nebuchadnezzar king of Babylon, my servant; I have even put the wild animals at his service. (All the nations will serve him, his son and his grandson, until the time for his own country comes in its turn, when mighty nations and great kings will enslave him.) Any nation or kingdom that will not serve Nebuchadnezzar king of Babylon and will not bow its neck to the yoke of the king of Babylon, I shall punish that nation with sword, famine and plague, Yahweh declares, until I have destroyed it by his hand. For your own part, do not listen to your prophets, your diviners, dreamers, magicians and sorcerers, who tell you: You will not be enslaved by the king of Babylon. They prophesy lies to you, the result of which will be that you will be banished from your soil, that I shall drive you out, and you will perish. The nation, however, that is prepared to bend its neck to the yoke of the king of Babylon and serve him, I shall leave in peace on its own soil, Yahweh declares, to farm it and stay on it' (Jr 27:5-11). The relevance of this reference is confirmed also in the First Letter of Peter, where Rome is spoken of as the new Babylon (cf. 1 P 5:13) and where, notwithstanding this, obedience to its sovereign and governors is recommended (1 P 2:13-14).

The attitude of the new and definitive rest of Israel, which is the Church, is therefore modelled on that of the 'rest' which, at the time of exile, obeyed God and the prophet. Obedience to the king of Babylon is the condition for remaining 'peaceful' in one's own land; to go against the king of Babylon, at that moment, means to go against God and face the 'sword'. The Pauline theme of prayer for 'the king and those in power' (1 Tm 2:1-2) is also part of this prophetic tradition. In the letter Jeremiah writes to those in exile, God ordered them to build houses and dwell in them, to take a wife, have children, to seek the welfare of the country they have been deported to, and to 'pray to the Lord for it', because their welfare depends on that of the country (Jr 29:4-7). This must be done until the days of Babylon have passed. Babylon is an unconscious and occasional instrument of God's plan in favour of his people, to purify them. What is said does not serve to give a divine basis to the Babylonian power, which remains what it is, one power succeeding another in the various combinations of good and bad human powers which, in their turn, will be replaced. Deutero-Isaiah, a prophet who came after Jeremiah, keeping to the same line of vision, will shortly tell us that now God has subjected the kings to Cyrus the destroyer of Babylon, and that it is he who is now the instrument of his plans, and must be obeyed (cf. Is 41:1ff; 45:1ff). This explains why the same prophet alternates between invitations to obey Babylon and abuse against Babylon, together with forecasts on its inevitable downfall. The same ambivalent attitude is to be found in the authors of the New Testament concerning the new Babylon, which is Rome. But the important thing is that all the authors of the New Testament agree about what Christians should do in such a situation, that is, obey, unto martyrdom if necessary, as Christ did. The idea of placing the existing political power on a divine basis was as far from Paul's mind as giving a divine basis to the power of Babylon was from Jeremiah's. The Apostle, following the line of the prophets, gives a divine basis more to the obedience of Christians to the state than to the state authority; he establishes the duty to obey the state rather than the right of the state to be obeyed.

But the text of Romans 13 does not reflect

only an Old Testament prophetic tradition; it also reflects an *evangelical tradition* and precisely what Jesus said about the tributes: 'Pay Caesar what belongs to Caesar – and God what belongs to God' (Mk 12:17). This statement is implicit in our text, where Paul tells us to give to each his due: 'taxes to the one whom tax is due' (Rm 13:7). This is going a step further than the prophets of the Old Testament and obedience to governing powers appears as a particular aspect of what the Apostle calls obedience to the Gospel. The Kingdom of God came with Jesus and it came in a way very different to what his contemporaries expected. It is a Kingdom that cannot be identified with governing power; it is of a different nature, as it is not of 'this world'. It follows that belonging to this Kingdom is not incompatible with belonging to and obeying an earthly kingdom, just as belonging to and obeying an earthly kingdom is not incompatible with adhering to this new Kingdom. In a certain sense, it could be said that the Apostle's main intention in Romans 13 is not that of telling Christians they *must* obey the state, but rather, that they *can* obey the state.

The Gospel has brought about a whole new situation which, to be accepted, demands a deep conversion on the part of the chosen people. The conviction rooted in the heart of every Hebrew person of the time, that foreign power usurps God's rights over Israel and is therefore against God, no longer holds. St Paul came from the very group of Pharisees who, in the Gospel, ask Jesus whether it was permissible to pay taxes to Caesar or not, hoping he would say it was not (cf. Mt 22:15). Paul himself actually says that in Judaism he outstripped most of his Jewish contemporaries in his limitless enthusiasm for the traditions of his ancestors (cf. Ga 1:13-16). He who had personally experienced conversion from law to grace (cf. Ph 3:7ff.) also personally underwent a second conversion, linked to the first, which was the psychological conversion from hostility to obedience towards the foreign political domination of Israel. This submission and loyalty towards the state are secondary but coherent consequences of the passing from law to grace, from circumcision to non-circumcision; in brief, from the Old to the New Testament. It is no use arguing that Paul was a Roman citizen, which could have favoured his positive attitude. It has been seen that the same attitude is to be found in Peter's First Letter and in writings which came after Paul, when the Church had begun its own negative experience of political power.

Taken in its true historical context, the Pauline text on obedience to civil authority is deeply innovative: we are dealing with obedience to what is new and to change which is the most difficult of all obediences. It is a lacerating transition to another type of humanity. Not all have obeyed the Gospel, the Apostle cries (cf. Rm 10:16; 1 Tm 1:8), meaning by 'obedience to the Gospel' not only and not so much obedience to the *content* of the Gospel, but rather and above all, obedience to the *fact* of the Gospel, that is, to the new situation that arises from the simple existence of the Gospel.

Obedience to authority, as formulated by Paul in Romans 13:1-7, far from favouring the maintenance of the *status quo*, is on the contrary the obedience required at times when deep changes are taking place. It is the obedience which tends not so much to support the old regime, as to recognise the existence of a new one and submit to it. This is how Paul's words sounded then to the Christians who were listening. This obedience is not found so much on the idea of a 'constituted order', be it natural or divine, but rather on the perception of the actual and living will of God, in the light of the Gospel.

In this prophetic and evangelic interpretation, the state fits perfectly into the category of those earthly affairs whose authority and laicality are affirmed by *Gaudium et Spes* of Vatican Council II. This Constitution says 'they are endowed with their own stability, truth, goodness, proper laws and order' by the very circumstance of their having been created, while at the same time stating that they remain dependent on God and subject to his judgement' (cf. GS 35-36).

I mentioned conversion and obedience to what is new. Christians were faced with the necessity of such obedience and conversion when, because of the barbaric invasions and the sack of Rome, they found themselves having to pass from one order of things to another, leaving behind them the Empire of Rome into which they had been by then well integrated. This was a repetition of the drama and bewilderment experienced at the beginning with the passing from the Jewish world to the Roman one. People again thought of the end of the world and it took another man of Paul's stature, St Augustine, to pacify consciences and urge them to keep striving, reminding them that in the changed historic context the Kingdom of God is not Caesar's kingdom, that 'God's City' is not identified with man's and can therefore outlive all the vicissitudes of the latter. A similar type of obedience and conversion to what is new probably exists again today, in the face of the big historical changes brought about by the end of traditional 'Christianity' and of some profound changes introduced by the Council. I wonder if God finds us more ready to obey than he found the Christians of the fifth century?

5. OBEDIENCE TO GOD IN CHRISTIAN LIFE

After this little parenthesis on obedience to civil authority, necessitated by the authoritativeness of Romans 13:1-7, and the misunderstandings this text is exposed to, let us now take a closer look at how to imitate Christ's obedience. At first glance an objection arises: what relationship can exist between the obedience of Jesus and our obedience if the ultimate terms of the obedience apparently change? The obedience of Jesus consisted in doing the will of the Father, whereas the obedience asked of us believers consists, as we have seen, in obedience to the Gospel, that is, to Christ. The answer is obvious: the will of the Father is now precisely that we obey his Son! Having perfectly fulfilled the will of the Father, Christ is now, also as man, the very personification of the will of God. His life and words are the concrete form that the living will of God has taken on for us. Jesus, says the Letter to the Hebrews, 'learnt obedience, Son though he was, through his sufferings; when he had been perfected, he became for all who obey him the source of eternal salvation' (Heb 5:8-9). In obeying the Father, Christ became the cause of salvation for all those who now obey him!

The will of Jesus is the will itself of God! Obedience to Christ is not obedience to an intermediary, but to God himself. With the coming of the new Covenant, obedience to the Gospel is the new shape that obedience to God has taken on.

But is it still possible and meaningful to talk of obedience to God, after the living will of God, manifest in Christ, has been completely expressed and objectified in a series of laws and hierarchies? Is it permissible to think that, after all this, there are still 'free' expressions of God's will to be accepted and fulfilled? If it were not so, nothing new would have flourished in the Church in these twenty centuries. We, however, can see that they have been filled with new things: new institutions, new vocations, new ways of living. Monachism, for example, came from obedience to the Gospel. One day Anthony went into a church in Alexandria in Egypt and heard the following being proclaimed: 'Go and sell all that you have, give it to the poor and then follow me'.[1] He took these words of the Gospel to be an order which God was addressing directly to him at that moment and he became a monk. The Franciscan Order also arose from a similar obedience to the Gospel. One day, at the beginning of his conversion, Francis of Assisi entered a church and heard the priest proclaiming the Gospel words: 'Take nothing for your journey, neither staff, nor hav-

---

[1] St Athanasius, *Life of Anthony* 2; cf. PG 26, 841C.

ersack, nor bread, nor money; and do not have a spare tunic' (Lk 9:3). He, too, felt this to be a command addressed personally to him by God at that moment and he exclaimed: 'This I want, this I ask, this I wish to do with all my heart!' and thus began his new way of life.[2] St Francis himself says in his Testament that his Order was born in that moment. 'After the Lord had given me friars – he wrote – no one showed me what I should do; but the same most high Lord revealed to me that I should live according to the way of the Holy Gospel'.[3]

If the living will of God could be captured and thoroughly and definitely expressed in a series of laws, norms and institutions, in an 'order' instituted and defined once and for all, the Church would end up paralysed. The rediscovery of the importance of obedience to God is a natural consequence of the rediscovery, started by Vatican Council II, of the charismatic and spiritual dimension of the Church (cf. the Constitution *Lumen Gentium*), and of the supremacy of the word of God in the Church (cf. the Constitution *Dei Verbum*). In other words, obedience to God can be understood only when it is clearly affirmed – as in *Lumen Gentium* – that 'the Holy Spirit guides the Church to the whole truth, it unifies it both in communion and ministry, instructs and directs it through

[2] Cf. Tomaso da Celano, *Vita prima* 22.
[3] *Testament* 14.

various hierarchical and charismatic gifts, adorns it with its fruits and constantly renews it and leads it to perfect harmony with its Spouse' (LG 4). Only by believing in the present and specific 'Lordship' of the Risen Christ over the Church, only by being deeply convinced that also today, as one of the psalms says, 'Yahweh is speaking, the God of gods, and will not be silent' (Ps 50), then and only then are we capable of understanding the necessity and importance of obedience to God. Obedience is listening to God who talks in the Church through his Spirit, who illuminates the words of Jesus and of the whole Bible, conferring authority on them and making them channels of the living will of God for us. Obedience to God and the Gospel was necessarily put a little in the shade, at least at the level of conscious reflection, when the Church was thought of above all in the terms of an institution, a 'perfect society', furnished from the beginning with all the means, powers and structures required to lead people to salvation without the need of any other specific and timely intervention by God. From the moment when the Church is again clearly seen as 'mystery and institution' together, obedience returns again to being as it was for St Paul, not only obedience to the institution but also to the Spirit, not only to men, but also and first of all to God.

But just as in the Church institution and mystery are united and not opposed to one another, we must now show that spiritual obedience to God rather than detracting from obedience to visible and institutional authority actually renews it. It strengthens and vivifies it to the point that obedience to man becomes the criterion for judging whether obedience to God exists or not and whether it is genuine or not. In general, obedience to God comes about like this. You feel flashes of the will of God in your heart; this is 'inspiration' which usually springs from the word of God listened to or read in prayer. The source of a certain thought is unknown to you, but it is there like a frail bud which can very easily be suffocated. You feel you are being 'questioned' by that word or inspiration; you feel it is asking something new of you and you say 'yes'. It is still a vague and confused 'yes' as to what has to be done and how it should be done, but clear and firm in substance. It is like receiving a sealed letter that you welcome with all its contents, thus making your act of faith. Thereafter, the interior clarity perceived at the moment of inspiration disappears; the reasons, so clear at first, become confused. Only one thing remains, and you cannot doubt this even if you want to: that one day you received an order from God and you answered 'yes'. What should you do in such circumstances? All the reflections and discernment possible are of no use. This inspiration does not come from the 'flesh', that is, from your intelligence, and you cannot therefore find it again through your intelligence; it came from the 'Spirit' and can only be found again in the Spirit. However, the Spirit no longer talks, as at first, directly to your heart. He is silent and refers you to the Church and her instituted channels. You must place your call in the hands of your superiors or of those who in some way exercise a spiritual authority over you, and believe that if it is from God he will make his representatives recognise it as such. At this point the experience of the Magi comes to mind. They set out on their journey, but in the meantime the star had disappeared. They had to go to Jerusalem and question the priests from whom they learnt their precise destination, that is Bethlehem! After this humble search, the star reappeared. They were thus to be a sign also for the priests of Jerusalem.

Hence it can be seen that it is possible to disobey even when 'obeying'. This happens when we take refuge in obedience to man in order to avoid obedience to God. A person feels the will of God upon him, a call that demands a change and a break with the past, with one's work, office... But he is not ready; he is afraid of saying 'yes' because he does not know where he is going to end up. So he places himself in the hands of his superiors who, knowing nothing about this will of God, will assign him to one of the many mansions and usual places among religious. He did right to place himself in the hands of his superiors in obedience, but this should have been done after informing them of the will of God he feels upon him. How many saints would not be saints if they had not done so? How much poorer would the Church be if, in the past, they had all limited themselves to obeying always and only what their superiors asked!

But what should be done when conflict arises between the two obediences and the human superior asks you something different or opposed to what you believe God wants from you? Just ask yourself what Jesus did in such circumstances. He accepted the external obedience and submitted himself to man and in so doing he did not deny obedience to the Father, but rather he fulfilled this obedience, which is exactly what the Father wanted. Without knowing or wanting it, sometimes in good faith and at other times not in good faith, men — as with Caiaphas, Pilate and the crowds — become instruments so that the will of God, not theirs, may be accomplished. Yet this is not an absolute rule: the will of God and his freedom may demand that a person obeys God rather than man, as with Peter before the order of the Sanhedrin (cf. Ac 4:19-20).

Some will object that such obedience to God is easy. God cannot be seen or heard and can be made to say what we want... This is true; but if someone is capable of letting God command him to do what he will, then he is all the more capable of letting man, that is, his superior, command him to do what he will! Scripture offers us a yardstick to help us distinguish between true and false obedience to God. It says that Jesus 'learnt obedience through his sufferings' (Heb 5:8). The measure and criterion of obedience to God is suffering. When your whole being shouts: 'God, you can't ask this of me!' and you realize that he wants just 'that'... and you are faced with his will as if it were a cross on which you must stretch yourself, then you discover how serious and real and daily this obedience is and how far it goes beyond every monastic rule. Isaiah tells the reason why obedience is 'learnt' – that is, experienced – through suffering, because God's thoughts are not our thoughts and his ways are not our ways, for the heavens are as high above earth as his ways are above our ways... (cf. Is 55:8-9). To obey God, making his thought and will ours, we have to die a little each time. In fact our first thoughts are different to God's, not just sometimes, as if by chance, but every time, by definition. Truly, to obey is to die. Here we discover the ascetic or 'negative' value which obedience to God holds; we learn how doing the will of God helps us in its turn not to do our own will. There is nothing that kills the human will so much as coming into direct contact with the will of God, because the divine will 'is something alive and active; it cuts more deeply than any two-edged sword! It can seek out the place where the soul is divided from the spirit' (cf. Heb 4:12). There is no possible escape from the word of God; it 'falls' on you as the sun falls on a wanderer in the desert where there is no shade in which to seek protection. However 'blind' obedience to man may be, it always allows for mental reservation because we know that the human will is not the last lap from which there is no 'appeal'; there is always the possibility (no matter how hidden) of 'having recourse' to God and complaining to him. But when we are dealing with God, who can we appeal to? There is no way out here: the human will must die; we cannot hum and haw! Let us look at Jesus. Let us look at him in Gethsemane when he is faced with having to say his 'yes' to the will of the Father; this was his 'agony', not the one before Pilate and the Sanhedrin. The acceptance of the will of man was, in comparison, much easier.

Obedience to God requires, each time, a real and true conversion. There is a page in the Bible that is like a poem on 'obedience and conversion' and which is worth listening to again, at least in part, because as word of God it is worth more than any human consideration. Moses is talking to the people and says: 'If you *return* to Yahweh your God, if with all your heart and with all your soul you *obey* his voice... then Yahweh your God... will have pity on you... you will *obey* the voice of Yahweh your God and you will put all his commandments into practice... Yahweh will delight in your prosperity... if you *obey* the voice of Yahweh your God, by keeping his commandments... if you *return* to

Yahweh your God with all your heart and soul' (Dt 30:2-10). The same formula applied to the love of God is applied to obedience; it must be done 'with all one's heart and with all one's soul'.

We must therefore state that it is, on the contrary, relatively easy to obey man and much more difficult to obey God. Man being man asks only for human things which are within his range and reason. God may ask for superhuman things which involve the death of reason. No human superior could have asked Abraham to leave his land and set out for an 'unknown' country, but God did; no man could have asked him to immolate his son, but God did. No man could have asked Mary what God asked her... But let us look at a few examples that are close to us. Today you had to carry out an order given by your superior which seemed unreasonable to you, dictated only by a whim and the superior's unpredictable and stubborn character. You hear someone talking about obedience to God and you exclaim: 'It is a thousand times easier to obey God than man!' But is this certain? God, this evening, is commanding you to 'love' your superior and you begin to fear a little because you know you are going to have to ask his pardon or, at least, confess. Let us consider another little example valid for both community and family life. Someone has taken or exchanged or tampered with an object belonging to you – a peace of clothing or something else in your use. You have firmly decided to point this out and get back what is yours. No superior tries to stop you. But then, without seeking it, the word of Jesus hits you with force, or opening the Bible you find it there as though by chance in front of you: 'Give to everyone who asks you and do not ask for your property back from someone who takes it' (Lk 6:30). You clearly understand that these words will not hold always and for everyone, but in this precise circumstance they hold for you; you are faced with a good opportunity to show obedience, and if you fail to show it you'll feel that you've missed out on a chance to obey God.

We can always obey God. We might have to obey visible orders and authorities only every now and then – to obey orders of a certain seriousness, maybe only three or four times in our life; but there are numerous obediences to God. The more we obey, the more numerous God's orders become, because he knows that the most beautiful gift he can give us is what he gave to his beloved Son Jesus. When God finds a person determined to obey him, he takes the life of that person in his hands, like the helm of a boat or the reins of a horse. Not just in theory, but in reality, he becomes 'Lord', that is, he who 'rules' and 'governs'. One could say that minute by minute he defines the gestures and words of that person, his way of making use of his time, everything. The person ends up behaving like a good religious subject of other times, who asked his superior's permission, or 'obedience' as it was once called, for every little thing.

There is nothing mystical or extraordinary in this; it is something open to all those who are baptised. It consists in 'presenting the question to God' (cf. Ex 18:19). I may decide by myself to make or not to make a journey, to do a job, to make a visit, to buy something, and once I have decided, pray to God for a good outcome. But if love of obedience to God grows in me, I'll first ask him, by the simple means of prayer that is at everyone's disposal, if it is his will that I make that journey, do that job, make that visit, buy that object, and then I'll act or not. But whatever the decision, it will be an act of obedience to God and no longer a free initiative of mine. It is clear that normally I shall hear no voice in my short prayer and I shall not be told explicitly what to do, or, at least, that this is not necessary to make my action an act of obedience. In so doing, I have submitted the question to God. I have emptied myself of my own will. I have renounced deciding for myself and I have given God the chance to intervene in my life if he so wishes. Whatever I now decide to do, based on the ordinary criteria of discernment, will be obedience to God. Just as a faithful servant never takes an order from an outsider without saying, 'I must first ask my master', so the true servant of God undertakes nothing without saying to himself, 'I must first pray a little to know what my Lord wants of me!' The will of God thus penetrates one's existence more and more, making it more precious and rendering it a 'living sacrifice, holy and acceptable to God' (Rm 12:1).

If this rule of 'presenting' the question to God is valid for the little things of everyday life, it is much more so for the big things, such as the choice of one's vocation: whether to marry or not to marry, whether to serve God in matrimony or in the consecrated life. The word 'vocation' itself, seen on the part of God, means call, whereas seen on the part of man, in a passive sense, it means to answer, that is, obedience. In this sense, the vocation is the fundamental obedience in life, that which realizes baptism and creates a permanent state of obedience in the believer. Those who marry must also do so 'in the Lord' (1 Co 7:39), for obedience. Matrimony thus becomes obedience to God in a liberating and not in a constricting sense, as is the case when one marries to obey one's parents or for some other necessity. It is no longer an exclusively personal choice which is presented to God only on second thoughts so that he might bless and approve it. It is a choice made with him in filial obedience to his will, which is certainly a loving will. When difficult situations present themselves it is no small difference to be able to say that this is God's will, that the choice was not made alone, and therefore God will not fail to give his help and grace.

This spirit of obedience helps us to overcome the difficult situations that we meet in every vocation or to make the most of them, as they too, are part of the saving will of God. God, says St Gregory the Great, 'at times admonishes us with words and at other times with actions', that is, with events and happenings.[4] There is an obedience to God – often among the most exacting – which consists in simply obeying situations. When we see that difficult situations, which may even seem absurd and spiritually harmful, do not change in spite of all our efforts and prayers, we must stop 'going against the grain' and look on them as the silent but resolute will of God for us. Experience shows that it is only after saying a whole-hearted 'yes' to the will of God, that such situations of suffering lose the anguishing power they have over us.

Furthermore, we must be ready to defer everything to do God's will: work, plans, relationships… Jesus deferred his teaching, ceased all activity and was not put off by the thought of what would happen to his apostles or the scandal that was about to break out because of him. He did not worry about what was going to happen to his word, entrusted as it was to the memories of poor fishermen. Not even the thought of his mother, whom he was leaving alone, held him back. His was really a 'blind, silent and deaf' obedience. He says in a psalm,

[4] *Hom. in Evang.* XVII, 1; cf. PL 76, 1139.

'I hear nothing, as though I were deaf, as though dumb, saying not a word. I am like the one who, hearing nothing, has no sharp answer to make' (Ps 38:14ff). What St Basil loved to call 'the irremovable and prompt obedience due to God' or obedience 'without excuse, prompt and irremovable', shines in the most marvellous and insuperable way in the life of Jesus.[5]

The most beautiful ending to a life of obedience would be 'to die for obedience', that is, to die because God says to his servant, 'Come!' and he comes. This was the way Moses died… 'There, in the country of Moab, the servant of Yahweh died as Yahweh decreed' (Dt 34:5). It was a great act of obedience for Abraham to renounce the 'son of the promise' at God's command but it was also a great act of obedience for Moses to renounce the 'promised land' at God's command. 'This is the country which I shall give to your descendants', God said to Moses on Mount Nebo, 'I have allowed you to see it for yourself, but you will not cross into it!' (Dt 34:4). The obedience of Moses is less remote from us than might at first be thought. It is in fact the same type of obedience one faces when God asks one to let someone else conclude a job and reap the reward for something one has been doing all one's life; and the same as when God calls someone to change role, or even calls

---

[5] St Basil, *De bapt*. 1; cf. PG 31, 1524-1529.

him to himself when he would still seem too young to die.

This is an obedience that has to be faced dramatically by a mother or father when one of them is recalled by God through a fatal illness while their children are still at a tender age and in need of their parents. Such an obedience, carried out in a spirit of faith by a Christian parent, can become a source of great blessings for those very children and a more precious and fruitful inheritance than life itself.

Real and concrete obedience to God is not simply the privilege of religious in the Church but it can be practised by all baptised persons. Lay people have not got a superior in the Church to whom they owe obedience, at least not in the sense that religious and clerics do. They have, however, a 'Lord' to obey! They have his Word! From its remote Jewish origin the word 'obey' means 'to listen' and in particular to listen to the Word of God. The Greek term for obedience in the New Testament (*hypakouein*) literally translated means 'to listen carefully' or 'pay attention', and the Latin word 'obedientia' (from *ob-audire*) means the same thing. Both listening and obeying interlace in this mournful lament by God which we find in the Scriptures:

Israel,
if only you would *listen* to me...!
My people would not *listen* to me,

Israel would not *obey* me.
If only my people would *listen* to me!
If only Israel would walk in my ways!
At one stroke I would subdue
    their enemies...
Turn my hand against their opponents'
(Ps 81).

In its original significance, therefore, obedience means submission to the Word, recognising its real power over us. It is easy therefore to understand how a rediscovery of obedience must be kept in mind while we are in the process of rediscovering the Word of God in the Church today. You cannot cultivate the Word of God without also cultivating obedience. Otherwise, you become disobedient *ipso facto*. Disobedience (*parakoneia*) means listening carelessly, with distraction. We could say it means listening in a detached or neutral way without feeling in any way obliged to act on what is being listened to and thus reserving one's own power of decision. The disobedient are those who listen to the Word but, as Jesus says, do not act on it (cf. Mt 7:26). It is not so much that they do not act on it as that they do not even think about acting on it. They study the Word but without the idea of having to submit to it; they dominate the Word, in the sense that they are masters of the tools of analysis, but they do not want to be dominated; they want to maintain that neutrality proper to every scholar with regard to the object of his science. On the contrary, the way of obedience is open to those who have decided to live 'for the Lord'; it is a need that is released by true conversion. Just as the Rules to be observed are given to a newly professed religious, so a newly converted Christian to the Gospel, in the Holy Spirit, is given this simple rule: 'Be obedient! Obey the Word!'

6. OBEDIENCE AND AUTHORITY

I have said that obedience to God is something we can 'always' do, at every instant. It is also, however, the kind of obedience we can all do, both subjects and superiors. It is usually said that one has to obey in order to learn how to command. This is a much deeper principle than mere common sense. It means that the true source of Christian spiritual authority lies more in obedience than in the office itself. The centurion in the Gospel says to Jesus: 'For I am under authority myself, and have soldiers under me; and I say to one man, "Go", and he goes; to another, "Come here", and he comes; to my servant, "Do this", and he does it' (Lk 7:8). The meaning is this: as the centurion is subject to, that is, obedient to his superiors and in the long run to the emperor, he can give orders that have the authority of the emperor himself behind them. His soldiers obey him because he in his turn obeys and is subject to his superior. This is what happens, the centurion thinks, between Jesus and God: since Jesus is in communion with God and obeys God, he has God's authority behind him and can thus command his servant to heal and he will be healed, he can command the illness to leave him and it will do so. It is the strength and simplicity of this argument that draws the admiration of Jesus and makes him exclaim that he has never found such faith in Israel. The centurion has understood that the authority and miracles worked by Jesus come from his perfect obedience to the Father.[1] The centurion does not make his authority over the soldiers depend so much on his having been appointed centurion by the emperor – in other words, he does not make it depend so much on the institution or title – as on being actually subject to the emperor. He does not make it depend so much on the office itself, as on the way and spirit with which he exercises it. He could be one of the many centurions in a state of rebellion and mutiny, but if he were, how could he ask his subjects to obey him? We know that this is what Jesus also did. He did not make his authority and the fact that all obeyed him depend so much on his dignity and title of Son of God, as on the fact that he carried out, moment by moment, the will of the Father: 'He who sent me is with me, and has not left me to myself for I always do what pleases him' (Jn 8:29).

To conceive authority as obedience means not to content oneself with the bare authority, but to seek also the authoritativeness that can only come from the fact that God is behind you

---

[1] Cf. C.H. Dodd, *The Founder of Christianity*, New York 1970.

and supports your decision. It means drawing near to that type of authority which radiated from Christ's actions and made people say: 'What authority have you for acting like this?' 'He taught them with authority' (Mk 1:22.27; 11:28; Mt 7:29). The people of that time knew many types of authority; Judaism was full of 'authority', yet Jesus' authority is seen as something new, something never before seen. We are in fact dealing with a different type of authority, a real and efficacious 'power' which is not just nominal or official; an intrinsic power and not just an extrinsic one. Even today the world is full of all kinds of authority, but very few with authority also possess authoritativeness. Communities and families are in great need of this type of spiritual authority. When an order is given by a superior or a parent who habitually tries to live in the will of God, who has prayed and has no personal interest to defend, but only the good of the subject or son, then the very authority of God becomes the counterpart of that order and decision. If disagreements arise, God then says to his representative what he said to Jeremiah: 'For look, I have made you into a fortified city, a pillar of iron, a wall of bronze... they will fight against you but will not overcome you, for I am with you' (Jr 1:18-19). If there is a crisis of obedience in our world, it is perhaps first of all because there is a crisis of authority, of this kind of authority.

This does not mean attaching less importance to the institution or office, or making the subject's obedience depend entirely on the degree of the superior's spiritual authority or authoritativeness. This would obviously be the end of all obedience. It simply means that whoever exercises authority must rely as little as possible and only as a last resort on the title or office he holds, and as much as possible on the union of his will with the will of God, that is, on obedience. The subject must not question himself or pretend to know whether the superior's decision conforms with the will of God or not; he must presume that this is the case. The title and office must suffice for him. By creating that office and placing that particular person in charge, God has already expressed his will for him. The same observation comes from all sides: obedience to God and the Gospel is good and it is the fruit of the Spirit if it instils in the heart the desire to obey also the representatives of God: authority, rules, superiors. The opposite situation is suspicious. Obedience to superiors is the visible sign of obedience to God just as love of one's neighbour is the visible sign of one's love for God. The first commandment remains the 'first' commandment, because the source and reason of all is the love of God; but the criterion on which this is judged is the second commandment: 'How can you love God whom you do not see, if you don't love the brother you see?' (cf. 1 Jn 4:20). If you don't obey the authority instituted by God, that is, those whom the Risen Christ has placed at the head of the Church, how can you say you obey the Risen Lord? However, it was necessary where obedience is concerned, as it was for charity, to throw light on the first commandment so as to preserve the 'second' commandment. The danger of the secularization of obedience is just as strong as the danger of the secularization of charity. The first commandment is 'You will love God'; the second is, 'and your neighbour as yourself'. If one loves one's neighbour disregarding the first commandment, that is, without any reference to God, we have what has been defined as 'the religion of the second commandment', a horizontal religiousness which could be just pure philanthropy. The same could be true for obedience even if in this case it would be a question of institutionalization rather than secularization. Obedience in this case is not given to the will of God but to detached images of it, maybe from a spirit of discipline, but more often out of pure habit. Obedience is done not on the newness of the Spirit, but in the oldness of the letter.

7. MARY, THE OBEDIENT

Before ending our reflections on obedience, we can now joyfully contemplate Mary, the living icon of obedience, she who not only imitated the obedience of the Servant but who lived this obedience with him. St Irenaeus writes: 'In parallel, (that is, parallel with Christ, the new Adam), the virgin Mary too is obedient when she says: "Behold, I am the servant of the Lord, let it happen to me as you have said" (Lk 1:38)... Just as Eve, by an act of disobedience became the cause of death for herself and the whole of humankind, so Mary by an act of obedience became the cause of salvation for herself and for the whole of humankind'.[1] St Irenaeus found in obedience the central point on which to base, on the one hand, the parallelism Jesus-Mary and, on the other hand, the antithesis Eve-Mary. In all three of the texts where this point is dealt with, it is on the grounds of obedience that Mary places herself side by side with Jesus and sets herself in opposition to Eve.[2] St Irenaeus had clearly understood the nucleus of St Paul's doctrine, expressed in Romans 5:19, and he extended it coherently to Mary and through her to

[1] *Adv Haer*. III, 22, 4.
[2] Cf. *Adv. Haer*. V, 19, 1; *Epideixis* 33.

the Church. In so doing he was the first to apply the doctrine of obedience to the Church. Where obedience is concerned, Mary acts as the linking point between Christ and the Church. Her obedience was an exemplary and prototypical imitation of Christ's which, in turn, is a model for the whole Church. It is known in fact that for Irenaeus, as indeed for all the tradition after him, the expression 'the new Eve' signifies at the same time both Mary and the Church: Mary, in a personal or typical sense; the other, the Church, in a general sense to the extent that in particular cases it is often even difficult to distinguish which of the two is being spoken of.

As we have here the first sketch of Mariology we must say that Mary enters the theological reflection of the Church as the Obedient. This is her personal prerogative, which is her due, and which more than anything else sets her side by side with Christ. Vatican Council II reasserted this view, quoting St Irenaeus' principal statements. Among other things it says that Mary, through her obedience, 'cooperated in the salvation of man', that beneath the cross she became through her obedience and faith 'mother by grace' and the Church's model (cf. *Lumen Gentium* 56, 61, 63).

I said at the beginning that it is relatively easy to discover the nature of Christian obedience: it is sufficient to see on which basis of obedience *Scripture* defines Christ as the obedient. I should now add that it is sufficient to see on which basis of obedience *Tradition* defines Mary as the obedient. Mary, St Irenaeus has told us, is obedient when she says: 'Behold, I am the Lord's servant, let it happen to me as you have said'. 'As through the work of a disobedient virgin', says St Irenaeus, 'man was wounded and, having fallen, died, in the same way, through the work of a Virgin obedient to the Word of God, he received life anew'.[3] Mary certainly also obeyed her parents, the law and Joseph. However, it is not this obedience that St Irenaeus is thinking of, but of her obedience to the word of God. Her obedience is the exact antithesis of Eve's disobedience. But – again the question – who was it that Eve disobeyed to be thus called the disobedient? Certainly not her parents, as she had none, and neither her husband nor any written law. She disobeyed the word of God! As Mary's 'fiat' is set side by side (in Luke's Gospel) with the 'fiat' of Jesus in Gethsemane (cf. Lk 22:42), so, St Irenaeus says, the obedience of the New Eve is set side by side with the obedience of the New Adam.

Let us reflect a little on this obedience of Mary to the word of God. 'With the words "Behold, I am the Lord's servant"', writes Origen, 'it is as if Mary were saying: I am like a tablet which is to be written on; the writer may write whatever he wishes, let the Lord of all do what he wills with me'.[4] He compares Mary with the wax tablet

[3] *Epid.* 33.
[4] Origen, *Comm. in Luc.*, fragm. 18; G.C.S. 49, p. 227.

used at the time for writing on, to show Mary's absolute docility. Mary offers herself to God as a clean page on which it is still possible to write anything one wishes; she gives back to God that absolute freedom he had over her right up to the instant in which she was created, when she was still only 'a thought of his heart' and he could have done whatever he wished with her, without her consent. 'The word of Mary', writes Schürmann, 'has always been of fundamental importance in pious reflections; it has been taken as the apex of all religious behaviour before God as it is the highest expression of passive availability together with active readiness'.[5]

Mary's obedience does not end with the Annunciation; that was, in a certain sense, only the beginning. During the Presentation in the Temple there took place for Mary something similar to what took place for Jesus during the baptism in the Jordan. On that occasion, through the word of the Father, the Messianic vocation became precise and clear in Jesus' conscience – in so far as this was a human conscience – as a vocation to be a Suffering Messiah, to be the rejected Servant of Yahweh, Jesus answered in obedience, thus renewing his 'Here I am'. During the Presentation, Mary's vocation, through the words of Simeon ('and a sword will pierce your soul too'), became precise and clear as the vocation to be the mother

---

[5]H. Schürmann, *Das Lukasevangelium*, 1982, *ad loc*.

of a contradicted and rejected Messiah, that is, as a hard and painful vocation. Mary too answered in silent obedience. Little by little she extended her 'yes' to the point of embracing everything it involved, even the cross. What is said of Jesus in the Letter to the Hebrews, 'that he learnt obedience through his sufferings' (Heb 5:8), can also be said of Mary. St Irenaeus implicitly applies these words to Mary, when he says that she too, made perfect, 'became the cause of salvation for humankind'.[6] Such an affirmation, that Mary through obedience became the 'cause of salvation for herself and for mankind' must not appear exaggerated and out of place. There was, in fact, only one obedience on Calvary, only one 'yes' said by both Son and Mother. Mary's 'fiat' was united to that of the Son, like the drops of water poured in the wine in the chalice become only one blood and only one 'drink of salvation'.

The obedience of Mary, from the moment of her 'fiat' at the Annunciation, is easily exposed to the danger of being made trifling, commonplace or merely devotional. To understand her 'fiat' in all its tremendous seriousness it is necessary to apply the category of contemporaneity to Mary, as illustrated by S. Kierkegaard in *Exercise of Christianity*. Mary was the only true 'contemporary' of Christ, in an even deeper and more radical sense than this philosopher ever

---

[6] *Adv. Haer.* III, 22, 4.

imagined. We believe in the things that actually took place, but Mary believed in what was taking place, while they were taking place. Mary obeyed 'in a situation of contemporaneity', not like us who see the facts at a distance of two thousand years after much verification, confirmation and explanation. We know what came after; but for Mary it was the first time such things had taken place and it was all so out of the ordinary and so dangerous! She was to become a mother before being married. Mary was certainly aware of what was written in the law: 'If the accusation that the girl cannot show evidence (to her husband) of virginity is substantiated, she must be taken out, and at the door of her father's house her fellow-citizens must stone her to death' (Dt 22:20-21). There was no human pretext for Mary to hold on to, no point of reference, other than God and his word; there was no explanation for her. We would need to put ourselves in Mary's place in order to appreciate the greatness of her obedience, but no one can ever really do this since it is impossible to repeat what happened only once in history.

What a lot we have to learn from the obedience of the Mother of God! Most times when we ask Mary's help, it is not so as to do God's will, but to change it. During her life on earth she would certainly have recited or listened to the verse of the psalm, addressed to God, which says: 'Teach me to do your will' (Ps 143:10). We should learn to say this the way she did.

8. 'HERE I AM, I AM COMING'

I am convinced that in order to overcome the present crisis of obedience in the Church, it is necessary to fall in love with obedience, because whoever falls in love with obedience will then easily find the way to practise this virtue. I have tried to throw light on a few points to help in this task: the example of Jesus, of Mary, our baptism... But there is one thing that speaks to our hearts more than all the rest and that is God the Father's favour and delight. Obedience is the key to God's heart. When Abraham came back from Mount Moriah, God said to him: 'I will shower blessings on you... All nations of the earth will bless themselves by your descendants, *because you have obeyed my command!*' (Gn 22:18). The tone of these words makes us think of one who has had to hold back long and with difficulty but who can, at last, freely pour out what is in his heart. It is like when gates are opened and the water from a dam pours down into the valley below. In all the generations right down to ours the wave of Abraham's obedience and that of God's blessing spread out to us. This is repeated with

Jesus on an infinitely higher level: because Jesus became obedient to death, the Father raised him high and gave him the name which is above all other names (cf. Ph 2:9-11). The favour and delight of God the Father is not a metaphorical expression, lacking in real meaning; it is the Holy Spirit! As Peter says in the Acts of the Apostles, God gives the Holy Spirit to those who obey him (cf. Ac 5:32). During the baptism in the Jordan, the Father, acknowledging the obedient Servant in his Son Jesus, proclaims his 'delight' and 'places' his Spirit on him (cf. Mt 3:17; 12:18; Is 42:1).

If we want to enter into God's favour and delight, we too must learn to say, 'Here I am!' This little expression resounds throughout the whole Bible. It is among the simplest and shortest in human language but among the most dear to God. It expresses the mystery of obedience to God. Abraham said: 'Here I am! (*Hineni*)' (Gn 22:1); Moses said: 'Here I am!' (Ex 3:4); Samuel said: 'Here I am!' (1 Sam 3:1); Isaiah said: 'Here I am!' (Is 6:8); Mary said: 'Here I am!' (Lk 1:38); Jesus said: 'Here I am!' (Heb 10:9). It sounds like a roll-call during which those called one by one answer 'present!'. These men really answered God's 'roll-call'! The Bible is particularly fond of this little expression, putting it also into the mouths of inanimate creatures: 'He calls them *(the stars)* and they answer, "Here we are", and they shine to delight their creator' (Ba 3:35). But among all the others in the Bible one

'Here I am!' is missing, and it was this missing 'Here I am' that marked man's destiny forever. When, after Adam had sinned, God called him, perhaps to pardon him, instead of answering 'Here I am' Adam went and hid himself (cf. Gn 3:10).

Psalm 40 describes a spiritual experience which can help us to form a 'resolution' at the end of this meditation. One day, full of joy and gratitude for the benefits of his God ('I waited, I waited for Yahweh, then he stooped to me...; he pulled me from the seething chasm...'), the psalmist, in a true state of grace, asks himself what he could do to respond to such goodness: should he offer holocausts, victims? He immediately realises that this is not what God wants of him; it is too little to express what is in his heart. At this point it is revealed to him that what God wants of him is a generous and solemn decision to do, from that moment on, what God asks of him, to obey him in everything. Then he exclaims:

> Here I am, I am coming.
> In the scroll of the book it is written of me,
> my delight is to do your will;
> your law, my God,
> is deep in my heart.

We know who took these words to heart before us. Now it is our turn. The whole of life, day by day, can be lived under the sign of the expression: 'Here I am, I am coming... to do your will, God' (Heb 10:7). We do not know what a certain day, a certain meeting, a certain job holds in store for us. We are certain of one thing only: that, whatever the situation, we only want to do the will of God. None of us knows what the future holds for us; but how wonderful it is to go towards it with these words on our lips: 'Here I am, I am coming to do your will, God'.